Verses written on the Alameda at Ampthill Park.

Jeremiah Holmes Wiffen

The BiblioLife Network

This project was made possible in part by the BiblioLife Network (BLN), a project aimed at addressing some of the huge challenges facing book preservationists around the world. The BLN includes libraries, library networks, archives, subject matter experts, online communities and library service providers. We believe every book ever published should be available as a high-quality print reproduction; printed on- demand anywhere in the world. This insures the ongoing accessibility of the content and helps generate sustainable revenue for the libraries and organizations that work to preserve these important materials.

The following book is in the "public domain" and represents an authentic reproduction of the text as printed by the original publisher. While we have attempted to accurately maintain the integrity of the original work, there are sometimes problems with the original book or micro-film from which the books were digitized. This can result in minor errors in reproduction. Possible imperfections include missing and blurred pages, poor pictures, markings and other reproduction issues beyond our control. Because this work is culturally important, we have made it available as part of our commitment to protecting, preserving, and promoting the world's literature.

GUIDE TO FOLD-OUTS, MAPS and OVERSIZED IMAGES

In an online database, page images do not need to conform to the size restrictions found in a printed book. When converting these images back into a printed bound book, the page sizes are standardized in ways that maintain the detail of the original. For large images, such as fold-out maps, the original page image is split into two or more pages.

Guidelines used to determine the split of oversize pages:

• Some images are split vertically; large images require vertical and horizontal splits.
• For horizontal splits, the content is split left to right.
• For vertical splits, the content is split from top to bottom.
• For both vertical and horizontal splits, the image is processed from top left to bottom right.

John Britton, Esq.

With Mr. Rogers's best regards.

Printed by order of the Duke of Bedford
in compliment to Lord Holland.

VERSES

WRITTEN ON

THE ALAMEDA.

VERSES

WRITTEN ON

THE ALAMEDA

AT AMPTHILL PARK.

———•———

By J. H. WIFFEN.

———————

" HERE THEN IS THE TRUE PARNASSUS, CASTALIA AND THE MUSES: IN THE WALKS
AND SHADES OF TREES THE NOBLEST RAPTURES HAVE BEEN CONCEIVED. HERE
POETS HAVE MADE THEIR VERSES, ORATORS THEIR PANEGYRICS, HISTORIANS
GRAVE RELATIONS, AND THE PROFOUND PHILOSOPHERS HAVE PASSED THEIR
LIVES IN REPOSE AND CONTEMPLATION. PARADISE ITSELF WAS BUT A KIND OF
NEMOROUS TEMPLE." EVELYN.

———————

LONDON:

PRINTED BY JAMES MOYES, TOOK'S COURT, CHANCERY LANE.

1827.

WRITTEN ON

THE ALAMEDA

AT AMPTHILL PARK.

———◆———

By J. H. WIFFEN.

————————

' HERE THEN IS THE TRUE PARNASSUS, CASTALIA AND THE MUSES: IN THE WALKS
AND SHADES OF TREES THE NOBLEST RAPTURES HAVE BEEN CONCEIVED. HERE
POETS HAVE MADE THEIR VERSES, ORATORS THEIR PANEGYRICS, HISTORIANS
GRAVE RELATIONS, AND THE PROFOUND PHILOSOPHERS HAVE PASSED THEIR
LIVES IN REPOSE AND CONTEMPLATION. PARADISE ITSELF WAS BUT A KIND OF
NEMOROUS TEMPLE." EVELYN.

LONDON:

PRINTED BY JAMES MOYES, TOOK'S COURT, CHANCERY LANE.

1827.

TO

HENRY RICHARD VASSALL,

LORD HOLLAND,

THESE VERSES ARE INSCRIBED,

WITH SENTIMENTS OF

DEEP RESPECT AND ADMIRATION,

BY

THE AUTHOR.

At the entrance of the town of Ampthill, in Bedfordshire, a Grove, consisting of four rows of trees, extending nearly half a mile in length, has been planted by LORD HOLLAND, for the future recreation of the inhabitants; an example well worthy of imitation by other opulent proprietors, and by civic corporations. It is matter of rational regret, that so obvious a source of salubrious and pleasurable enjoyment should not have been more generally created in the vicinity of our towns and cities. The College walks at Cambridge and Oxford, and a few others, may, indeed, be cited as exceptions to this strange neglect; but in regard to what EVELYN would quaintly call "the architecture of nemorous temples and cathedrals," we are far behind our continental neighbours. It is true that every foreign city has not Boulevards like Paris and Rouen; but in France there seems to be no great number of cities and towns of consequence without a decorative public Grove; and in Spain, *every* considerable town has its ALAMEDA, where the better classes are accustomed to assemble in the afternoon, for amusement and refreshing shade. These places are called *Alamedas*, from *Alamo*, a name common to both the elm and poplar, the trees which are generally, though not uniformly, selected to shade such spots. The planted walk at Ampthill consists of lindens; and the happiness of the choice will be evident to every one who has paced the noble lime-grove at the back of the Mansion in Ampthill Park; which presents, for the admiration of the visitant, a long and lofty aisle of verdure, of singular beauty and solemnity, and losing none of its soothing effect upon the mind in summer by the mellifluous sound of myriad bees amongst the blossoms. The taste of the Planter has projected a suitable stone entrance to the ALAMEDA which is the subject of the following Lines;—over the gate of which, in accordance with the Spanish title and historical associations of the spot, are to be sculptured the arms of Castile and Arragon; Ampthill Castle having been the residence of KATHARINE, daughter of FERDINAND and ISABELLA of Spain, whilst her divorce from HENRY THE EIGHTH was pending. In commemoration of this circumstance, the late EARL OF UPPER OSSORY erected in his Park at Ampthill an elegant octagonal Cross, well known to the topographer by the inscriptive Verses of HORACE WALPOLE.

WOBURN ABBEY, June 30th, 1827.

VERSES

ON

THE ALAMEDA

AT AMPTHILL PARK.

—— Pia et alterius studiis operata Minervæ,
(Nam tenui donat victura volumina libro),[a]
Stat PHILYRA; haud omnes formosior altera surgit
Inter Hamadryadas; mollissima, candida, lævis,
Et viridante comâ et beneolenti flore superba,
Spargit odoratam latè atque æqualiter umbram. COULEII *Plantarum*, lib. vi.

I.

UNQUESTIONED let the column soar,
　　The vaulted temple rise to tell
Of deeds which after-times adore —
　　Where patriots lived, or freemen fell;
　　To meditative minds a spell
Is in the slightest record placed
　　To honour loved or laurelled names,
　　In duty to the generous aims
Of genius and of taste.

II.

The piles by our first EDWARD reared,
   In grief for his connubial loss ;[b]
The urn to SHENSTONE's heart endeared,
   And brave PHILIPPA's trophied Cross ;
   Sweet PEMBROKE's Pillar, gray with moss,
In sound of Eamont's murmuring fall ;
   And CLIFFORD's fountain, — are to me
   Like haunted shrines — there's poesy
And pathos in them all !

III.

But towers, but temples have their own
   Mute griefs, besieged by lorn decay ;
And if Heaven's thunder spares the stone,
   'Tis mined by envious Eld away.
   Nature alone subdues to play
The warring churl, — her forests fade,
   But to renew for him who loves
   The influence of the breathing groves,
Life, music, flowers, and shade.

IV.

Thus, HOLLAND, shall thy verdant limes,
  Though oft seared rudely, flourish still,
And, raised, transmit to distant times
  The image of thy frank good-will !
  There, let but Fancy have her fill
Of thought, and thou shalt hear the talk
  Of groups blithe-hearted as the best
  That charm, when Vesper tints the west,
Seville's own elmin-walk.

V.

There Mirth, there Wit shall lance his shaft,
  And when their wilder voice is mute,
Mild echo to thy halls shall waft
  The warblings of some Doric flute ;
  No warm debate, no harsh dispute,
Shall vex the Dryads' ears, beyond
  Ingenuous Beauty's tones, that chide
  The kiss, half granted, half denied,
To lips as pure as fond.

VI.

There Youth shall urge his vacant sport,
    There Age relax his thoughtful brow,
And harassed Toil indulgence court,
    And Care grow glad, unconscious how ;
    And if, as elder bards avow,
Scenes where the vanished Great have strayed,
    Still claim their gentle spirits, there,
    In the still twilight, shall repair
Full many a storied shade.

VII.

Forms that in olden time adorned
    The jewelled court, the tented camp,
That life for nobler virtue scorned,
    Or watched by fancy's charmed lamp ; —
    De Mowbray, with his Red-cross stamp,
Who won, by Pity's generous lure,
    The lion to his leash in fight ;[c]
    And, with his princely bride, the Knight
That fought at Azincour.[d]

VIII.

BEAUCHAMP and amorous SEYNT-AMAND,
 Whose knightly scutcheon none could blot,
Borne pure in many a dauntless stand
 'Gainst Gascon Earl and stalwart Scot:
 Well knew the archer as he shot,
From far, Sir ALMARIC's gifted glove,
 And taxed the bezants on his shield,
 To prove how well the shafts could yield
Praise to his ladye-love.

IX.

Nor last, that wondrous Youth, to whom
 The lute was lovely as the sword,[e]
Who found on Zutphen's plains his doom,
 By an admiring world deplored;
 And at his side, the Friend that scored
Such numbers with his curtelax grim,[f]
 That the foe shunned it as the mace
 Of that Unearthly One, whose face
Heaven's bolts have rendered dim.

X.

Yes, they shall come, and with them glide
 The Sweet and Sad of other days;
SIDNEY's dear Sister, the fond pride
 Of SPENSER's strains, and JONSON's praise;
 And, soothed perchance by WALPOLE's lays,
And OSSORY's Pillar that prolongs
 Her fame, there KATHARINE too shall rove,
 And lose, in thine Elysian Grove,
All memory of her wrongs.

XI.

What though for her there pass not by
 The proud and portly alguazil,
The water-carrier's languid cry,
 Or mantled Matador's appeal,
 Nor touched guitar, nor seguidille
Danced to the clinking castanet, —
 No veiled Señora's flirting fan,
 Nor sun-kissed fruit-girl's darted scan
From eyes of sparkling jet; —

XII.

Yet groups and customs shall ye trace
　　Of happier arts and brighter times,
And courtesies that give not place
　　To the forced growth of warmer climes;
　　For ne'er beneath thy shading limes
Shall the hired Bravo stand, to aim
　　At patriot worth, nor Monk command
　　Deeds such as now make Spanish land
A synonym for Shame.

XIII.

No, ne'er! but in their stead the wise
　　And dauntless lineage of the free, —
Some FOSCOLO, whose lettered sighs
　　Are all for bleeding liberty;
　　Or olive-crowned ARGUELLES, — he
Whose image like a key unlocks
　　The portal of proud thoughts and aims,
　　Glorious as to our theme the names
Of MACKINTOSH and Fox.[g]

XIV.

Some mild Licentiate, whom thine arm
    Has saved perchance from bigots' cells;[h]
Some Bard, in whose pure breast the charm
    Of memory's evening sunshine dwells;[i]
    Whilst, listening to the distant bells
That sound from Milbrook's rural tower,
    By Wit, by Song, by Loveliness
    Made blithe, THOU too ofttimes shalt bless
The beauty of the bower!

XV.

For fresh with ripening years, and green
    The boughs shall spread, the umbrage fall,
As in poetic page is seen,*
    Within the' alluring Castle-wall,
    Where lavish Idlesse deals to all
Delicious ease, divine repose;
    And rosy dreams that none may tell,
    But they that walk thy woods or dwell
In happy Vallombrose.

* Vide Thomson's " Castle of Indolence."

XVI.

No fairer Grove shall have o'erspread
   The crowd that to the *Laughing Sage*[k]
Gave ear, or bowed the approving head
   O'er THEOPHRAST's didactic page;
   Not that, where PLATO would engage
His guests on themes, pure, grave, and high;
   Nor where sweet CLIO with her Style
   Prompted THUCYDIDES to smile
On deeds that ne'er can die.

XVII.

No lovelier Grove, if Poet's vow
   Still float to deep DODONA's shrine,
Shall song to earth call down, than now
   My tuneful prayers create of thine;
   Its Guardians be the sacred NINE!
Its voice by night, its guest by day,
   The warbling nightingale and dove;
   Its spirit peace, its look be love,
Its breath perpetual May!

XVIII.

Farewell! in childhood's careless prime
   It soothed to list the hum of bees,
To pluck wild flowers, and lisp wild rhyme
   Beneath thine immemorial trees,[1]
   Sweet Ampthill! and for joys like these
'Tis fit I strike an idle chord,
   To sing these rising Groves of thine,
   And in thy grateful service twine
One laurel for thy Lord!

NOTES.

NOTES.

Note A, page 9, line 3.

———— *Pia et alterius studiis operata Minervæ,*
Nam tenui donat victura volumina libro.

In illustration of this reference to one of the admirable qualities of the lime-tree, it may be mentioned, that a volume, made of the inward bark, was brought to the Count of St. Amand, Governor of Arras, in 1662, for which eight thousand ducats were given by the Emperor: it contained a work of Cicero, *De Ordinanda Republicâ, et de inveniendis Orationum Exordiis;* an unpublished treatise, which, after having been the greatest rarity in the Library of Cardinal Mazarine, must now, I imagine, enrich that of Vienna. Slips of the same material were also, as we learn from Ovid and Horace, used by the ancients to bind the garlands of roses and other flowers with which they crowned themselves at their convivial entertainments:

Ebrius incinctis *philyrâ* conviva capillis

Saltat.   Ov. *Fasti*, lib. v.

Displicent nexæ *philyrâ* coronæ.

Hor. lib. i. *Carm.* 38.

COWLEY's lines, although somewhat amplified, are thus very happily rendered by APHRA BEHN:

> " For pious use and noblest studies fit,
>
> MINERVA here might exercise her wit,
>
> And on the lasting vellum which it brings,
>
> May in small volumes write seraphic things."

Note B, page 10, stanza 2.

The piles by our first EDWARD reared,

In grief for his connubial loss, &c.

The Gothic crosses at Northampton, Leighton, and Waltham, with several others, as at Lincoln and Charing Cross, were erected by EDWARD THE FIRST, to mark the stations where the body of Queen ELEANOR nightly rested, on its way from Nottinghamshire to Westminster; a tribute by no means too costly for his own gratitude and the devoted heroism of the Lady who had sucked the poison from his Syrian wound. The inscription on Miss DOLMAN's urn at the Leasowes, is known to every body. An elegant stone cross was raised by RALPH, Lord NEVILLE, on the spot where the battle took place, to commemorate the victory of Red Hills, which was won by Queen PHILIPPA, under his conduct, over DAVID, King of Scots, in 1346. PEMBROKE's Pillar, near Brougham Castle, is celebrated by Mr. ROGERS, in the " Pleasures of Memory;" and at Woodstock is a spring flowing into a sequestered basin, to which the beautiful ROSAMOND DE CLIFFORD has bequeathed her name. When, seven or eight years ago, I visited the Countess's Pillar, in Westmoreland, I was grieved to find the capital thrown

down, and lying by the way-side : this ought not to be, for the little column
was erected by one of the most accomplished and heroic women of her age,
and to the virtues of a RUSSELL. This was MARGARET, daughter of FRANCIS,
the second Earl of Bedford, who, notwithstanding her many amiable endowments,
was much neglected by the Earl of Cumberland, her husband. He was chi-
valrous and brave; but was content to sport away his youth and fortune in
tilts and tourneys, as fantastic champion to the capricious " Virgin Queen;"
whilst his Lady, whom LODGE truly terms " a woman of extraordinary merits,"
was left in privacy and poverty at Brougham or at Skipton Castle, to chronicle
her hours in a melancholy diary, and to educate her daughter, the promising
ANNE CLIFFORD; who, indeed, repaid her cares with the tenderest affection. Although high-spirited by nature, she bore the slights of her Lord with exemplary
patience ; and it is doubtless to this feature of her character that DANIEL alludes,
when he says to her, in his Epistles,

> " And whereas none rejoice more in revenge,
>
>   Than women use to do; yet you well know,
>
>   That wrong is better checked by being contemn'd,
>
>   Than being pursued ; leaving to Him to avenge,
>
>   To whom it appertains : wherein you shew
>
>   How worthily your clearness hath condemn'd
>
>   Base malediction, living in the dark,
>
>   That at the rays of goodness still doth bark.

> " And this note, Madam, of your worthiness
>
>   Remains recorded in so many hearts,
>
>   As time nor malice cannot wrong your right,
>
>   In the heritage of fame you must possess,—

> You, that have built you, by your great deserts,
>
> Out of small means, a far more exquisite
>
> And glorious dwelling for your honoured name,
>
> Than all the gold that leaden minds can frame."

The Earl of Cumberland learned, late, to estimate her worth; and on his death-bed had many compunctious visitings, on account of his neglectful treatment of her.

Note c, page 12, stanza 7.

> *DE MOWBRAY with his Red-cross stamp,*
>
> *Who won, by Pity's generous lure,*
>
> *The Lion to his leash in fight.*

At the time of the Norman Survey, the manor of Ampthill belonged to NIGEL DE ALBINI, a potent Baron, who, at the battle of Tinchbrai, in Normandy, slew the horse of ROBERT CURTHOSE, and brought the Duke himself a captive to King HENRY. His son, ROGER DE MOWBRAY, possessing, as well as HUGH DE ROSEL, the ancestor of the Earls and Dukes of Bedford, lands at Granville, in Normandy, was a joint benefactor with that Baron to the Abbeys of Caen, giving his lands there to the Abbess of St. Trinity, when his daughter took the veil beneath her rule. He made two journeys to the Holy Land, where he was taken prisoner with GUY LUSIGNAN, King of Jerusalem, but was redeemed by the Knights Templars. As he was returning to England, a curious incident is stated to have occurred. In his journey, says the legend, through the vale of Sarranel, he was witness to a furious conflict between a dragon and a lion. Taking part in the singular quarrel, he slew the dragon; whereby the lion became so gratefully attached to him, as meekly to follow him into England to his castle. Ampthill passed by female heirs from the family of ALBINI to the BEAUCHAMPS and ST. AMANDS, of whom came ALMARIC DE SANCTO AMANDO, a warrior of great chivalry and prowess. He was made Governor of Bourdeaux by EDWARD I., and signalized himself in various expeditions which that Monarch undertook into Gascony and Scotland. His arms were, *Or*, frettée *sable*, on a chief of the second, three bezants.

Note D, page 12, stanza 7.

" *And, with his princely bride, the Knight*
That fought at Azincour."

Sir JOHN CORNWALL, afterwards Lord FANHOPE and Baron of Milbrook; to whom, in 1441, WILLIAM BEAUCHAMP DE ST. AMAND conveyed the manor of Ampthill. At a tournament at York he won the heart of ELIZABETH, sister of K. HENRY THE FOURTH, and at the battle of Agincourt fought bravely in the van, which was the station assigned him from his noted courage.

Note E, page 13, stanza 9.

" *Nor last, that wondrous Youth, to whom*
The lute was lovely as the sword."

In Houghton Park, which immediately adjoins that of Ampthill, the excellent MARY SIDNEY, Countess of Pembroke, had a noble Mansion, near the ruins of which a tree is pointed out, beneath whose boughs her brother, Sir PHILIP, the mirror

D

of pure chivalry and honour, is said to have written a part of his Arcadia. LYSONS has stated some considerations, that, in the eye of the biographer, may seem to disprove the fact; but with the visitant and poet the pleasing illusion may still be suffered to remain.

Note F, page 13, stanza 9.

> " And at his side, the Friend that scored
> Such numbers with his curtelax grim."

Sir WILLIAM RUSSELL, Baron of Thornhaugh, fourth son of FRANCIS, second Earl of Bedford. On the field of Zutphen, coming where Sir PHILIP SIDNEY lay so sorely wounded, Sir WILLIAM kissed his hand, and said with tears, " O noble Sir PHILIP! never was there man attained hurt more honourably than ye have done, nor any served like unto you*." To him, as his dear friend and comrade, the dying youth bequeathed his best gilt armour. So terribly in this celebrated action did Sir WILLIAM ply his curtelax, that the Flemings, says STOWE quaintly, " reported him to be a devil, not a man." A spirited painting of him, in the mêlée of battle, in the attitude and with the visage (so far as the portrait allowed) most conformable to this description, has recently been painted by Mr. COOPER for the DUKE OF BEDFORD.

Note G, page 15, stanza 13.

> " Glorious as to our theme the names
> Of MACKINTOSH and FOX."

For the sake of the subject alone, it may be necessary here to state, that

---

* Stowe, p. 737.

Sir JAMES MACKINTOSH is at this time an occupant of the Mansion at Ampthill Park, where the Noble Planter of the ALAMEDA passed his boyhood.

Note H, page 16, stanza 14.

" *Some mild Licentiate, whom thine arm*
Has saved perchance from bigots' cells."

Don LEUCADIO DOBLADO.

Note I, page 16, stanza 14.

" *Some Bard, in whose pure breast the charm*
Of memory's evening sunshine dwells."

SAMUEL ROGERS, Esq.

Note K, page 17, stanza 16.

" *No fairer Grove shall have o'erspread*
The crowd that to the Laughing Sage
Gave ear."

Both DEMOCRITUS and THEOPHRASTUS, as well as other philosophers, taught and lectured in the gloom of Groves. PLATO also entertained his auditors amongst his walks of trees, which were afterwards defaced by SYLLA, who cut them down to build forts against the Piræus. But he had another venerable Grove, planted near Anicerides with his own hands, where grew the celebrated palm-tree, under which he introduces SOCRATES discoursing with PHÆDRUS. And PLINY tells us, that

THUCYDIDES was reported to have compiled his noble history in the still recesses of the Scaplan Groves.—Vide EVELYN's *Sylva*, p. 313.

Note L, page 18, stanza 18.

" *It soothed to list the hum of bees,*
   To pluck wild flowers, and lisp wild rhyme
   Beneath thine immemorial trees."

At Ampthill, the author received a portion of his early education.

THE END.

LONDON:
PRINTED BY JAMES MOYES, TOOK'S COURT, CHANCERY LANE.

CPSIA information can be obtained
at www.ICGtesting.com
Printed in the USA
BVHW062316131221
623925BV00010B/251